Uncommon Sense:

One CEO's Tale of Getting in Sync

Uncommon Sense:

One CEO's Tale of Getting in Sync

Andy Kanefield and Mark Powers

ISBN-10: 0-615-29447-2 (paperback); ISBN-13: 978-0-615-29447-6 (paperback)

Printed in the United States of America.
Set in Clarendon and Today.
Book design by Karin Soukup; Illustrations by Dan Zettwoch.

This paper is made from regenerative eucalyptus fiber from a mill that is carbon neutral.

Published by Sync Press.
www.dialect.com

"When one tugs at a single thing in nature, he finds it attached to the rest of the world."

- John Muir

Table of Contents

You are about to pull back the curtain and get a quick glimpse at the world of Jack, CEO of Horizon Bank. As you do, you'll get to know a little about Jack and his management team. And you'll see how they go beyond common sense to apply what we're calling *uncommon sense.*

* **Note:** *As you read about Jack and his team you will have the option of interacting with the principles they are discussing as they address their business problem. While we recommend that you interact with the principles after each chapter, please feel free to read the entire book and then return to reflect on their application to your organization. Either way you choose to interact with the book, we do hope you apply it to your situation. Look for the blue notebook pages (like the graphic at left) for these moments of interaction.*

Horizon Bank

Our Cast of Characters

Jack
CEO of Horizon Bank

Austin
President of Horizon Bank

Pete
Chief Financial Officer (CFO) of Horizon Bank

Pauline
Chief Marketing Officer (CMO) of Horizon Bank

Stuart
VP of Human Resources for Horizon Bank

Kevin
Chief Operating Officer (COO) of Horizon Bank

Brian
Organization Development (OD) consultant

Lloyd Carter
Director, Horizon Bank; former Director, Liberty Bank

Thomas Pinkerton
Director, Horizon Bank

1

Out of Sync

Jack knew his run as CEO might be over and the thought put all his senses into overdrive. As he pulled his Lexus into his spot in the underground parking garage he could see the rough road ahead, but he was ready. Hard work always energized him. He didn't get to be CEO of one of the nation's largest banks because he was afraid of challenges.

As he got into the elevator, he decided to stop at the lobby before going up to the executive suite. He stepped out into the silent atrium and waved at the guards who were moving toward the bank of elevators. It was hours before opening time.

"It's just me, fellas," he called. Jack loved the solemn quiet of the bank lobby with its polished marble and brass. Even when it was full of people, it seemed majestic, even stately.

Back in the elevator he punched 24, thinking briefly of the trust department as he passed the 5th floor. It had grown exponentially in the past ten years. They hadn't been prepared for its growth. They should have been.

He stepped out into the reception area of the executive suite and headed to the boardroom. His executive assistant, Mary, wouldn't be here for another hour, and he wanted time alone to think. The boardroom in the early morning was his sanctuary.

Jack ran his hand over the smooth leather of the chair at the head of the table. His chair. He intended to keep it. In three months he would face the board again and be expected to deliver a growth plan. Horizon Bank had acquired Liberty Bank one year ago and the financial projections hadn't been met. In yesterday's meeting, the board members sent a clear message that they wanted an updated growth strategy for the next three years. Jack wanted to handle the next meeting well. It could mean his job.

He slowly circled the table, studying the large photos on the wall collected for the bank's 100th anniversary. He never tired of looking at them, never failed to draw inspiration from them. The first Horizon Bank was a small brick building on the edge of downtown. The founder had been a major force in the development of the city and people still remembered his name with gratitude. During the Great Depression, when banks were closing left and right, he kept Horizon open, reducing his own salary to a dollar a year and taking a streetcar to work.

So many changes in the thirty years Jack had been at Horizon. What changes would the next thirty bring? He had to think of a strategy that could adapt to a continually changing world and convey a sense of stability in these rocky times. He definitely did not want a further decline in their key metrics. The board had already hammered him about the bank's efficiency ratio and net interest income.

And there was Lloyd Carter to deal with – what a thorn he could be. Not that Jack wanted a rubber-stamp board. But Carter was a legacy board member from Liberty Bank who was opposed to the acquisition from the beginning and was the driving force behind the board's mandate.

Jack had assembled an outstanding team of senior leaders whom he trusted. *I need their input right now.* He grabbed a notepad from the sideboard, sat down, took out a pen, and wrote a memo asking his team for their thoughts on the board's growth strategy directive.

A few minutes later, Mary stuck her head around the door. "So this is where you are."

Jack sighed. Sometimes Mary could be too efficient. But he could never get irritated with someone who looked like Mrs. Santa Claus with her halo of white hair.

"You have an appointment with Pauline in ten minutes," Mary said. "Stephenson from Trust needs to talk to you about a major client who's gotten a little too eccentric. Legal found another minor glitch in the Collins contract, and Patrick from the *Times* wants an interview."

"Thanks, Mary." Jack stood. "Schedule Stephenson for one. Ask legal if they can handle the glitch without me and stall the *Times* for now. And could you put this memo into an email for me?"

Jack's chair creaked as he stretched back and stared at the ceiling, reflecting on the events of yesterday's board meeting. Spurred on by sudden inspiration, he pressed the intercom button and asked Mary to bring him the folder on acquisitions. He'd done acquisitions before and things had gone smoothly, but this time the pressure of the board's directive nagged at him. The bank had added 1,000 employees rather than 100 or even 200. He knew it was harder to connect people to your strategy when there was less personal contact with senior leaders.

He believed the maxim that "the leader is a reader," keeping a file of articles from a broad array of publications that caught his eye. If it was interesting, he clipped it or printed it out and gave it to Mary to file.

Leafing through the bulky file on mergers and acquisitions, he found a *Wall Street Journal* article on the Procter & Gamble (P&G) acquisition of Gillette. As he read the article, he wondered how well the cultures of these two banks were integrating. Gillette employees had to cope with a more rigid P&G culture. He frowned. After a year, are employees of the smaller, nimbler Liberty Bank seeing their new colleagues and the bank that Jack helped build as too slow and bureaucratic? What other cultural adaptations should both legacy organizations make?

All the operational issues and employee issues that arise after an acquisition had occupied everyone's attention for months. Now he had to address the directional issues. *How do I keep everyone moving in the same direction? How do I keep from feeling that all my time is spent herding cats?*

Maybe most importantly, what do our customers see today?

* **A unified bank with a strong sense of purpose, customer focus, and direction?**

* **Or a bank showing signs of a confused identity, presenting multiple and distinct identities and displaying conflicting ways of interacting with customers?**

How can Jack and his senior team get the organization in sync so it can grow?

Section I:

The System

2

Why We Do What We Do

Pete, the Chief Financial Officer (CFO) of Horizon Bank, was almost always the first member of Jack's senior team to respond to his memos. He was quick and efficient. He was also an imposing figure — tall, lean, and impeccably dressed.

"So, you got the memo," Jack conjectured as Pete entered Jack's office. Jack's office was a contrast to Pete's tidy, efficient one. Piles of letters and file folders were stacked throughout the room — neatly stacked, but stacked nonetheless. He liked to keep things in sight. His desk was a working desk with a large calendar, computer, and line of framed family photographs. A smooth, fist-sized rock served as a paperweight.

"I did," Pete acknowledged. "Is now a good time to talk about it?"

"Absolutely," Jack replied, moving from behind his desk to greet him. They sat at a small, oval table next to a bookcase jammed with reports.

"Jack, we can't grow if we don't know why we do what we do." Pete got right to the point. "Everyone else is concerned about the banking crisis, but I'm concerned about whether or not we know what business we're in. This credit crunch has clients calling us constantly, and our relationship managers are drinking Maalox for breakfast, lunch, and dinner."

Jack nodded. His stomach was feeling the tension too.

"I used to think banking was fairly simple," Pete continued. "We take in deposits and lend capital to qualified borrowers. But it seems like our account service time right now is spent more as therapists rather than bankers. Are we therapists or bankers?"

"Maybe we're both," Jack offered. "What I've noticed is when things are going well, we don't ask these broader questions because we're fat and happy in our success. It's when things turn sour that we tend to ask the more reflective questions like yours."

"Yeah, but don't we typically ignore them? I know I do. In a downturn, I'm asked to focus on cutting costs, not address that great organizational, existential question, 'Why do we exist?'"

"But, this could be a great opportunity to refocus on the basic purpose of the bank. We could show the board that we're not just thinking tactically, but we're reexamining all aspects of who we are. What do you think?"

"Maybe you're right."

"How would you answer that great existential question, 'Why do we exist?'" Jack asked.

"Well." Pete stumbled. "Here's what I know. We provide a valuable service. We exist to meet needs that our customers have."

"And, what are those needs?" Jack asked, holding his pen poised over his notepad.

"Our depositors clearly want a return on their investment," Pete began. "And our lending clients want access to capital at the lowest possible cost. But as we've talked to clients these past few weeks, I've realized there's more to it than financial return. I'm starting to look beyond the numbers and ask what the financial gains or losses do to them."

"Hold that thought for a moment. What do our employees think we're doing?" Jack asked. "I know that some of our employees look at their jobs as more than a paycheck. How do you think they view their role if they were to ask 'What are we doing?' of themselves?"

"I think most shareholders and employees believe the bank exists solely to make money. Personally, I think profit is only part of the story. No one, ultimately, works just to make money. It's what money does for a person that matters. It may mean a bigger boat, a new car, a feeling of security, the chance to pursue a business dream, or a feeling of superiority — but money, in my mind, is an instrument to get something else. It's a means to an end. I think our customers' concerns these last few weeks go far beyond the financial numbers. There's something deeper at work."

Jack nodded. He knew that businesses that overemphasize short-term financial measures and neglect a broader purpose miss opportunities to create value for clients. The longer he listened to Pete, the more he realized he was stuck. He didn't have a clear answer for why Horizon Bank exists.

He wrote "Why do we exist?" at the top of his notepad. Underneath he wrote the following questions while reading them out loud to Pete:

* **Do we exist to make banking simple for our customers?**
* **If this is why we exist, how does that help our customers?**
* **Do we exist to help our customers feel financially secure?**
* **Do we exist so our customers can live their dreams?**
* **Do we exist so our customers can be happier?**

"Pete, what happens if we, as an organization, don't have a common answer to this question?"

"People will create their own personal answer, I suspect," Pete replied tentatively.

"And what if the answers that employees provide don't fit with the best interests of other stakeholders?"

"I guess we have a problem," Pete suggested. "We might be working at cross purposes. If our services and processes don't deliver on our purpose — whether we've articulated one or not — we're wasting time and resources and our customers aren't getting the value they expect."

"So what are we saying?"

Pete's face transformed into a grimace he had seen earlier on Jack's face. "I guess we need to know what our purpose is."

Jack wrote "Purpose" on his notepad.
* **Purpose:** *Why do we exist?*

Use Jack's notepad to record thoughts about your organization's purpose.

3

Whom Do We Serve?

Pauline, Chief Marketing Officer (CMO) of Horizon Bank, was soft-spoken and firm in her opinions while, at the same time, she was open to re-examining her opinions. She had scheduled an early morning appointment with Jack to discuss her input on the growth strategy.

Taking off her designer reading glasses, she said, "Jack, my 30,000-foot assessment is that we need to have a laser-like focus on our key stakeholders and know what they value most."

She paused to offer Jack an opportunity to defend the bank, but he just replied, "Go on."

Pauline walked over to Jack's whiteboard and wrote the following list in big red letters:

* **customers**
* **potential customers**
* **employees**
* **shareholders**
* **vendors**
* **partners**
* **local communities**

"We already know that we have to meet the needs of all of these stakeholder groups," Pauline began. "But what I think we don't address well is the question, 'Is there a key customer group for the bank, and do we know what they value most?' Because if we don't meet the needs of that key customer group, we'll never be able to meet the needs of our other stakeholders.

"I read an article recently that was written by Sidney Winter of the University of Pennsylvania," Pauline continued. "Winter had studied the sensors of natural organisms that help them survive in the natural world and applied this knowledge to organizations. He learned that some moth species can detect the sonar of bats. To avoid becoming a bat snack, these moths are able to use evasive aerial maneuvers to escape. In the environment of the family living room, however, these same moths can't detect the sound of a rolled up newspaper whizzing toward them.

"Like nature's organisms, we need to have highly developed sensors that help us survive in a competitive marketplace. Horizon Bank's sensors need to be appropriate for our market, gathering useful information, and accurately detecting what is valuable to customers, employees, and shareholders. We need to promise something meaningful, verify that this meaningful service is delivered, and recognize stakeholders' changing needs so delivery can adapt as necessary. We don't want the bank to be the moth in the living room."

"Do we have a profile of our key customers?" Jack asked.

"Not a very good one," Pauline replied.

"That's step one," Jack shot back, irritated that his CMO didn't know their customers better. "If we don't have that we're a sitting duck ... or moth."

Pauline didn't laugh. She was embarrassed that she didn't have a better handle on the bank's customers. The board mandate had forced her to get back to fundamentals rather than putting out fires.

"Put together a research plan right away. We need to have something in hand when we talk to the board. And you should drive the project," Jack added. "Don't delegate it. It needs to have your ownership so that people move quickly on it."

"Right," Pauline responded.

Jack pulled out his pad and scribbled "Stakeholders" underneath "Purpose."

* **Purpose:** *Why do we exist?*
* **Stakeholders:** *Who are our key stakeholders and how do I make sure we're continually in sync with what they value?*

Use Jack's notepad to record thoughts about your organization's

key stakeholders and what they value.

4

How We Are Different

Thoughts of his conversation with Pauline lingered with Jack, but he hadn't the time to think much more about the bank's key stakeholders or the growth strategy until his commute the next morning.

Most days, Jack drove his car to the office since he needed it for client meetings. But on certain days, he indulged in one of his favorite activities — riding the train downtown. Ever since traveling throughout Europe during a college summer abroad program, he had loved taking public transportation. It was quick, efficient and a great opportunity to indulge in another of his favorite activities — reading.

As he bounced against his seatmate on an unusually bumpy train ride, he placed the *Wall Street Journal* across his lap and thought more about the bank's need for greater customer insights

The bank's offices were a ten-minute walk from the train station. Jack normally spent that time reviewing the purpose of each meeting on his calendar for the day. Today he churned the stakeholder question over and over as he stepped briskly through the crowd of commuters. Ideas flitted in and out of his mind as he thought about recent consumer insight reports Pauline's team had produced.

"Mary, call Pauline and have her come in here please," Jack barked as he walked into his office.

Ten minutes later, Pauline and Jack were sitting at the small conference table in his office.

"I've given our conversation more thought this morning on the way into the office. Let's assume that we don't know our key stakeholders very well. What do we know?" Jack asked rhetorically.

"Our customers don't see us as having any meaningful differences from any other bank," Jack answered himself. "We've emphasized fast service, but that's only because of our customer survey results. When we ask current customers why they bank with us, the most common reason is convenience. They either talk about our locations or our on-line services. So we've interpreted that as a green light to focus on speed of transaction delivery.

"What do prospective customers say?" he asked rhetorically ... again.

"First, they claim that they don't bank with us because we're not convenient to home or work. They also mention the inertia of being with the same bank for over 10 years."

"So are you saying the answer is to be more convenient?" Pauline asked.

"No, I'm not sure that convenience alone will be the primary driver of loyalty in the future. It seems that convenience is just the ante to stay in the game. It's the minimum we need to provide. But we need something more. Plus convenience is too easily mimicked."

Pauline waited for more.

"I'm worried about what we're learning," Jack continued. "The consumers that we're talking to want to have financial transactions and advice from trustworthy sources. That could be either through technology or people. This acquisition made us bigger, but did it make us better where it counts? By focusing on getting bigger, we are taking resources away from getting better at providing reliable counsel at all levels of the bank — from the teller to the boardroom.

"We have an opportunity to put a stake in the ground and claim that we're truly different," Jack added. "If we don't do it now, you and I may not be around to do it. We'll end up like all the other banks — vanilla in a sea of vanilla. We have the chance to be Rocky Road!"

Pauline chuckled. She was still uncomfortable because it felt like Jack was on her turf.

"The people we interview in our research are overwhelmed by the choices they have to make," Jack went on. "Not just in considering banking services but in every aspect of their lives. Look at the average grocery aisle. Barry Schwartz, in his book 'The Paradox of Choice,' wrote about strolling down the aisles of his local supermarket and counting 230 different soups with 29 different chicken soups. It's chicken soup for cryin' out loud!"

Pauline shook her head. She could relate. She was constantly annoyed by the number of options available for even the simplest of items. It slowed her down.

"There were 175 different salad dressings and 16 types of Italian dressing," he added, incredulous.

"Jack, I couldn't agree with you more," Pauline replied. "We need to give people a clear and authentic reason to choose us. We have to help our potential customers simplify their choices by having a compelling reason to choose us — one that we can consistently follow through on. One aspect of our growth strategy needs to be my upcoming meeting with our marketing consultants. We need to be able to describe to them what is different about the 'new' Horizon Bank. But will that differentiator, whatever it is, connect to where we're going as a bank and connect to our customers?"

"If you look closely at how we deliver," Jack answered, "we're not built to deliver trusted advice. We're built to provide quick and efficient transactions. And we seem to be moving even further toward the quick and efficient end of the spectrum. We have given operations carte blanche to use more automation and reduce personal contact."

"You know the data better than I do. Do you really think people are willing to trade efficiency and convenience for the type of relationship we're talking about?" Jack asked.

"Think about it this way," Pauline suggested. "You just talked about how overwhelmed people are with choices. The same is true for financial services. Most people don't enjoy the details of figuring out what is best for them and how they can keep from losing their retirement savings to the black hole of hidden fees. It can be complicated. People want experts they can trust."

"But even if being trusted advisors isn't the best way to differentiate the bank, you're onto something," Pauline added. "We need to come to an agreement on some signature strength and then retool so we can deliver it. That's the message we need to send to the board in three months."

Jack twirled his pen. "OK, marketing expert. Does this clear and authentic reason have to be something truly unique? We are a bank you know. Banks struggle with how to differentiate themselves all the time. We're not exactly known for figuring out how to stand out from the crowd."

"Our differentiator doesn't always have to be unique." Pauline put on her glasses, peering at him over the tops. "In a perfect world it would be, but at the very least it has to be something that no one else does as well as we do. And it has to be something that is important to our customers and potential customers. It has to engender loyalty."

Jack stood up and looked out the window. Far below on the street was a small, white moving truck. On the side panel was painted, "Two Men and a Truck — Movers Who Care." "So," Jack thought out loud, "these guys haven't carved out a niche as the only movers who care. They just claim that they care more."

Pauline inched over to the window. "You have great eyesight," she commented. "And yes, you're right. They are claiming they care more. And if they hire people who don't care or only care about getting a paycheck, that claim won't mean anything. In fact, it will do more harm than good."

"Then, once we know the reason customers should choose us, we weave it into everything we do. It becomes our DNA. It's our John Hancock. It's our signature. It's what we're known for," Jack mused aloud.

Jack took out his notepad and added another line to his notes.

* **Purpose:** *Why do we exist?*
* **Stakeholders:** *Who are our key stakeholders and how do I make sure we're continually in sync with what they value?*
* **Signature Strength:** *How are we different? What are we best at? What engenders the most loyalty from our customers?*

Use Jack's notepad to record thoughts about your organization's signature strength.

5

A Picture of the Future

While Jack still had moments when thoughts of the next board meeting made him tense up, he felt some comfort from knowing that he was getting good input about the growth strategy. There was a small sense of accomplishment at knowing more about what he didn't know.

His first meeting on Wednesday morning was with his president, Austin. Austin had been around banking all his life and facilitated the bank's annual strategic plan review. They sat in the overstuffed chairs in a corner of Austin's spacious office. Jack shared with Austin bits of his conversations with Pete and Pauline and his own concerns.

Abruptly Austin revealed that, "Others are concerned, too, Jack."

"What do you mean?" Jack asked with a hint of worry in his voice.

"They're not concerned about you. They trust you."

"Not everyone does." Jack tensed his jaw. "There's at least one board member—"

"True. Carter is a problem. But I think his influence is limited. He has influence but not enough to do irreparable damage."

"He still has a loud enough voice to do some damage."

"I'm thinking more about our own people. They're concerned that as an organization we're not sure where this acquisition has taken us. There's a sense that we don't know where we're going."

Jack leaned forward. That was not what he wanted to hear.

Austin continued, "My grandfather used to say that you can't focus on fog. Some of our people need to know where we're going. But right now there's no clarity about where we're headed or even hope to go.

"Think about what happened the last time you drove through fog. You slowed down or maybe even stopped ... because you couldn't see much further than the front end of your car. Or, you were on edge ... because sometimes the fog was so thick you couldn't see where you were at the moment, let alone the path ahead of you.

"Or maybe you made a bad decision even when you knew better ... like turning your lights onto high-beam when all that does is to reflect more light back at you, so you can't see your hand in front of your face."

Jack's frown deepened.

"I can tell that some of our people are slowing down because they don't know where we're headed. Others are just frustrated because they need to know what's next and they can't see what's ahead. Some are making bad choices because they feel like they need to try to do something in order to see better.

"All of these options are bad for the bank. We need clarity."

"What do you recommend?" Jack was holding his pen so tightly he was afraid it would snap.

"We need to send a message to the board that we have a clear picture of the future we're working toward – something people can attach to. I'm sorry to use this buzzword, but we need a vision."

"You know that a good percentage of our people are going to chafe at anything called a vision," Jack said. "It sounds so pie-in-the-sky. You do realize that we're bankers."

"I know," Austin continued, "but we have options for how we talk about it. We don't have to label it a vision – that's a discussion for another time. I'm more concerned about the need to have clarity about where we're going. It doesn't have to be a long-term vision. We just need to have something beyond today to focus on.

"We've talked about the future being bright and more prosperous, but that's not enough. We're expected to say that. Our people want to have a clearer, more concrete, tangible picture."

Jack nodded thoughtfully.

"And don't forget that Kevin and I have very different views about our direction with this acquisition," Austin added.

"I remember it well," Jack acknowledged, thinking of past clashes between Austin and his COO. "If we can't all agree on our direction, we could be in real trouble."

Jack suddenly recalled a *Wall Street Journal* article about Anne Mulcahy's turnaround of Xerox. Mulcahy always tried to, "Show employees what the company that survives will look like."

For Xerox, survival was the issue. While the bank's survival is not at risk, my survival might be. The principle Mulcahy pointed out was critical. For some employees, and even some customers, it isn't enough to know that the organization will be successful; they need to know what that success will look like.

Articulating this vision so that it comes to life and is compelling to people inside and outside the company is difficult. Yet we can't expect people to move together toward a future they cannot see.

As Jack walked back to his office, he thought about the direction he wanted the organization to go. He wondered whether the behavior necessary to get there was part of the fabric of the bank. On top of that, he had questions about the best way to reinforce that behavior as Horizon Bank continued to absorb Liberty Bank.

Back at his desk, Jack added to his notepad.

* **Purpose:** *Why do we exist?*
* **Stakeholders:** *Who are our key stakeholders and how do I make sure we're continually in sync with what they value?*
* **Signature Strength:** *How are we different? What are we best at? What engenders the most loyalty from our customers?*
* **Vision:** *Where are we going?*

Use Jack's notepad to record thoughts about your organization's future state.

6

Behavior that Leads to Success

On his drive to the office on Thursday morning, Jack thought about his upcoming meeting with Stuart, his head of Human Resources (HR). He needed Stuart's input on the bank's growth strategy. As head of HR, Stuart had been tasked with leading the bank's People Team. This team was responsible for, among other things, the bank's talent management program.

Stuart was a skilled facilitator and knew how to think about organizations in human terms. Stuart would have some interesting insight into what the growth strategy should be.

As soon as Jack walked into Stuart's office and the pleasantries were finished, Stuart began.

"I've had several discussions over the last few days that have led me to think that we may have to reinforce some new behaviors."

After drumming his fingers for a moment on the desk Stuart said, "I know that we did a cultural audit before the acquisition to make sure there was sufficient compatibility. We wanted to make sure that our colleagues from Liberty were clear about what our core values mean to us."

"And the audit went well," Jack interjected.

"But we did our audit with the assumption that our behaviors would stay the same and Liberty would adopt our values. But if we need to shift what or how we deliver services based on what our customers are telling us, our behaviors may need to change. I'm struggling with how to address that in some way through our core values. Our strategy isn't in sync."

"So, give me a concrete example," Jack asked.

"Right now, our values are, we're fast, we're ethical, we work in teams," Stuart replied.

"But what if we develop a picture of the future that requires more deliberate, thoughtful behavior," Stuart continued. "What if what people really want from the bank of the future is a trusted advisor? Being fast wouldn't be as important, would it?"

"We would probably still want to be fast, but not emphasize it as much," Jack acknowledged.

"Right," Stuart affirmed. "We would focus on being relationship-oriented and thorough rather than fast. We would want the bank to be a network of employees bound by a shared belief in the importance of delivering trustworthy advice, in which each person understood his or her role in delivering that advice."

Stuart and Jack were both green MBA grads during the Tylenol crisis of 1982. The coverage Johnson & Johnson got and the example the company set stayed with them.

Seven people had died after taking Extra-Strength Tylenol capsules laced with cyanide when CEO Rob Burke ordered a nationwide withdrawal of Tylenol products from store shelves and warned the public not to take any products they had already purchased. His first question, posed to his strategy team during the crisis, was: "How do we protect the people?"

Johnson & Johnson regained the public's trust by living the behavior it claimed to embrace in its credo — that its first responsibility is to "mothers and fathers and all others who use our products and services."

"We both saw the importance of living our values at Johnson & Johnson," Stuart continued. "We need to be sure we're doing the same thing, but I'm not sure we know who we are anymore."

"Let's assume that our values need to evolve. How do you recommend we promote different values throughout this network that you describe?" Jack asked.

"Well, I think the first principle is to recognize the desired behavior when we see it, celebrate it, and reward it," Stuart suggested. "We want to align our values with our unique identity as a bank. And we need to reinforce the behavior that helps us stay in sync."

"That sounds like formal programs to me," Jack responded.

"That's part of it. But you know how much I dislike having everything done by org charts and formal processes. It would also mean recognizing the informal networks that develop — the 'meetings before the meeting' where coaching and mentoring take place and alliances form. There is a place for formal coaching, mentoring, and recognition programs. But what happens around the water cooler is often at least as important as what happens around the conference room table." Stuart ran a hand through his hair. "What we don't want are statements of core values that don't match how we act. That's a formula for creating a Dilbert culture and derisive water cooler discussions."

Jack nodded.

"Values that aren't lived are, at best, mere shadows of what could be," Stuart continued. "At worst, they are hollow promises of behavior that leave disappointed stakeholders staring at meaningless words on posters in our hallways. And from a talent management perspective, we're always looking for people who not only get results but also achieve those results in a way that is consistent with our values. That helps us and provides some moral authority to suggest that people follow those we choose as leaders.

"And that can lead to some hard choices," Stuart added quickly. "We may need to replace some highly visible staff members with people who share and can live our values."

Jack wrote on his notepad as Stuart continued to talk about the importance of matching behavior to the future of the bank and the needs of customers.

* **Purpose:** *Why do we exist?*
* **Stakeholders:** *Who are our key stakeholders and how do I make sure we're continually in sync with what they value?*
* **Signature Strength:** *How are we different?*
* **Vision:** *Where are we going?*
* **Culture:** *What behavior is key to our success?*

Use Jack's notepad to record thoughts about your organization's core values.

7

Getting the Right Things Done

Back in his office, Jack pulled a stack of index cards from a drawer and wrote the salient points from each recent conversation with his team members about the growth strategy. He could feel the knot in his stomach flex its considerable muscle as he thought about the board's growth strategy mandate.

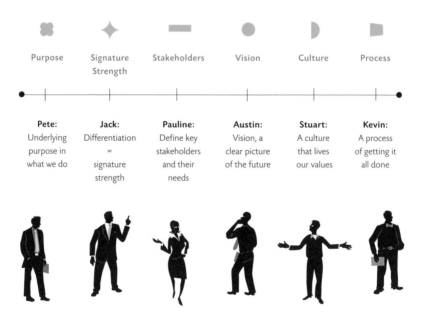

Purpose	Signature Strength	Stakeholders	Vision	Culture	Process
Pete: Underlying purpose in what we do	**Jack:** Differentiation = signature strength	**Pauline:** Define key stakeholders and their needs	**Austin:** Vision, a clear picture of the future	**Stuart:** A culture that lives our values	**Kevin:** A process of getting it all done

As he shuffled these cards around on his desk, he wondered how he was going to create a growth strategy that could take into account all of the issues he had discussed with his senior team. On his notepad he wrote:

* **Articulate our purpose and define our key stakeholders.**
* **Make sure our values and processes support our direction, purpose, stakeholder needs, and signature strength.**
* **Clarify what seems fuzzy so that we can build the "infrastructure" to deliver it.**
* **Build the "infrastructure" to deliver what we're clear on.**

Mary's voice came over the intercom. "Kevin would like to meet with you at 10:30. Does that work?"

"Yup. But tell Peterson I'll be 20 minutes late for lunch. Thanks, Mary. "

Kevin breezed in promptly at 10:30. He always seemed to be going 60 mph, even when he was standing still.

"Hey, Jack. Sorry to be so late responding to your memo. A hundred brush fires to put out – you know how that goes." He threw his pro-football-sized frame into the chair in front of Jack's desk. Jack winced, hoping it would hold him.

"I want your input on our growth strategy," Jack began. He briefly summarized his conversations with Pete, Pauline, Austin, and Stuart. "My challenge as I see it is to figure out how to deliver what we know we want to deliver and to build an organization that will deliver something that isn't clearly defined ... yet."

Here's what is set:

* Our direction: *I don't know how to describe it well, but we want to expand our reach and services. The how is still unclear.*
* Our purpose: *Why we exist. It's here. We just have to play a little bit to express it well.*
* Our values: *Most of our values still apply. We may need to refocus our attention from speed to depth.*

Here's what we don't have clearly defined:
* The needs of our key stakeholders.
* Our signature strength.

Here's where you come in. We need to develop operational procedures that work for all of this AND fill in the gaps as we go.

"You're right," Kevin interjected. "And we've got the board pressuring us for a growth plan with a huge expectation on their part that it will be operationally heavy. I can see why you're nervous."

Jack nodded, relieved that Kevin was so quick to grasp the problem.

"Of course, I'll need to work with everybody to clarify what all this means," Kevin continued. "And how we define that signature will affect how we operate — big time. I want our customers to see that we're built to deliver what we're promising. There is nothing more frustrating than mixed messages and inefficient operations! I want a clear connection between what we say and how we operate! It seems that our growth strategy needs to address these issues." Kevin ticked them off on his fingers:

* **How will we move toward our desired future?**
* **How will we build the culture we need?**
* **How will we deliver on our purpose in a way that meets the needs of our key stakeholders?**
* **How will we ensure that we are truly differentiated and what concrete things can we do to demonstrate how we're different?**

"Yes, that sounds spot on, Kevin," Jack affirmed, his spirits rising. He appreciated Kevin's ability to analyze what needs to be done and quickly make it operational.

"We've got our work cut out for us, Jack, but we can do it." Kevin stood up to leave and added, "It may be third and long, but we'll convert this one."

Use Jack's notepad to record thoughts about your organization's

key strategies that enable you to deliver value.

Section II:

From Confusion to Clarity

8

The Phone Call

Early on Tuesday morning, two weeks after the board meeting, Jack received a phone call from Thomas Pinkerton, a long-time board member of Horizon Bank. Pinkerton was universally respected in the business community and the retired CEO of a large manufacturing company. While he was no longer Chairman of the Board, his voice had the weight of that position.

"Jack, do you have a few minutes?" Pinkerton began.

"Always for you, Tom."

"I wanted to remind you that I'm behind you 100 percent. I have confidence in you and your team. You've got good business sense and your team respects you, which is key in my book."

"Thanks, Tom. I need a vote of confidence right now."

"I also wanted you to know that Carter is going to be pushing hard for change at the next board meeting." Jack groaned inwardly. "He continues to lobby other board members and, given enough time and a continued drop in share price, he could soon have the votes to remove you."

The discomfort in Jack's stomach intensified.

"Thanks for warning me. Any advice?"

"Whatever you and your team present, it has to speak to everyone in that board room. Each person has to find something in your plan that is the key to unlocking the bank's door to success. Listen, I've got to run. Call me later, and we can talk more if you like. I just wanted to reinforce the gravity of what we've asked you to do and let you know I'll do what I can to help you."

"Thanks, Tom. I appreciate it."

"Oh, and Jack, one more thing. While the plan needs to speak to each member of the board — that's hurdle number one — it's also important that it speak to your employees and customers. The plan has to come alive. I've really got to run. Talk to you soon."

"But, Tom..." *Click.* The phone went silent and so did Jack. *Reinforce the gravity? The knot in my stomach reinforces the gravity. And what did Tom mean that our growth strategy needed to speak to employees and customers? Am I supposed to print it up for the world to see in multicolored brochures? Am I supposed to create multimedia presentations?*

He slowly rose from his chair and started to pace. After a few minutes, he asked Mary to cancel his lunch meeting.

He then picked up the phone and punched in the number of one of his college roommates, Brian. Brian had a PhD in Organizational Psychology and worked for a multinational consulting firm. He was a consultant to a number of Fortune 500 CEOs.

"Brian, can you break free anytime today?"

"My lunch appointment just bailed on me so I've got two open hours."

"Can we meet at the club and play some racquetball?"

"You reserve the court, and I'll see you at 11:30?"

"See you there, Brian. And thanks."

"No problem. The exercise will help me make it through a marathon conference call I have this afternoon."

9

The Club

Jack realized as he put the towel to his face to dry off the sweat that he didn't exercise nearly enough. He was in decent shape, but he had begun to get a bit flabby and was winded after 15 minutes of racquetball. After an hour he was drenched and totally out of breath.

"So, Jack, you're pretty quiet. What's on your mind?"

"Two weeks ago we had our board meeting, and I was told to come up with a growth plan for the next three years. Our stock price hasn't met expectations since the acquisition and because the acquisition was my idea and my first major decision after being named CEO, several board members have lost confidence in me."

"That is a problem. What are you doing about it?"

"Well, I've asked for input from each person on my senior team, but they're all saying different things. They each have unique views on what will fuel our growth."

"How is that a problem?"

"Isn't that obvious? I want them to be united. We need to be in sync."

"Are their unique views mutually exclusive?"

Jack paused for a few moments. "I'm not sure. Maybe not. I know that some of the team have been talking to each other so their thoughts may be somewhat aligned. Although it sure feels like we're out of sync. Don't we all need to be focused on the same thing?"

"Fair enough. Let's schedule a time to look at their ideas closely to see how well they fit together. But first, let me suggest an alternative way to think about this. The parts of our body have unique views, too, on what is essential to grow. Yet, the parts work well together ... when we take care of them.

"The heart says, 'The key is to pump more blood,' while the lungs say, 'The key is to feed more oxygen.' You get the picture. The parts are complementary and each of them supports the whole. Being in sync doesn't mean that you have to see everything the same way."

"That makes sense. There are times when Jill and I are in sync on issues related to the kids, yet we are very different and have different perspectives."

"Exactly. From an organizational perspective each person is looking at the bank through his or her own filter. They experience the bank differently and they perceive the bank differently because of that filter ... it depends on how each person is wired." Brian closed his locker door.

"So, are we hard-wired? Or can we change our filters? Because sometimes I just want to say, 'Hey, see it my way or off with your head.' Jack slammed his locker door, and it bounced back and hit him.

Brian laughed. "Well, we're learning more and more about how we're wired, but it's a challenge to say what is permanent and what is 'plastic' as the neuroscientists like to say. For those of us who aren't experts, the key to remember is that even if certain aspects of our filters are plastic, we're always going to be interacting with people who have filters that are different than ours, and we have no right or opportunity to change their filters. And even if we did, changing the way we perceive the world is a long-term proposition."

"Brian, would you be willing to come and talk to the team about this? I want to take you up on your offer and sit down with you first and review the input so far. Then I want you to talk to my team about filters. I think that will help us. There might be a way we can use it with the board, too."

"I'd be glad to. It will be fun to work on something together other than your lousy backhand."

10

Jack's Epiphany

Jack and Brian agreed to meet at Brian's office to reduce the likelihood of being interrupted. Brian's office was filled with golf memorabilia that he had collected or bought. He was proudest of the autographed picture with Tiger Woods that was taken at a client's golf clinic. After Jack admitted coveting Brian's golf skills and collection, he got down to business.

"Brian, I brought my notes."

"So, let's see what we have here." Brian glanced through Jack's notepad and sifted through the index cards.

* **Pete:** *Underlying purpose in what we do*
* **Jack:** *Differentiation = signature strength*
* **Pauline:** *Define key stakeholders and their needs*
* **Austin:** *Vision, a clear picture of the future*
* **Stuart:** *A culture that lives our values*
* **Kevin:** *A process of getting it all done*

"So, Jack, why did you buy Liberty Bank?" Brian started.

"Good question." He frowned. "It seemed like a good opportunity to generate additional revenue for our stakeholders by expanding our reach through adding more locations. And Liberty had a well-developed technology platform that was scalable and they had successfully integrated this technology across all lines of business. They could point to metrics that showed significant improvement in customer capability because of their ability to integrate this platform.

"Simply put, we wanted to grow and provide better service to our customers. The banking industry is mature in many ways, and I believed, and still do, that being able to quickly adapt to customer needs is the way to win market share.

"But, as I mentioned to you last week, our financial results haven't met pre-acquisition expectations. So, the board has given us a mandate — develop a growth strategy for the next three years."

"OK." Brian leaned forward. "So do you think the board's expectation is reasonable?"

"I do think it's reasonable that we have a growth strategy. I'm not pleased with Carter's attitude. He gives off an 'I told you so' vibe.

"Because he was opposed to the acquisition?"

"Exactly. But, that's just my impression."

Brian spread the index cards across his desk. "So do you want to know what I see when I look at these cards?"

"Of course."

"First, the good news. Your team is right. Each of these perspectives can be part of your growth strategy."

"And the bad news?"

"The bad news is what you already know ... that you're not in sync. But not because your team members have different views on what will fuel your growth. It's because their different views aren't in sync yet."

"I'm not sure what you mean. Can you clarify that?"

"Sure. Let's start with the reason you bought Liberty. Your goal was to grow revenue while enhancing customer service, right?"

"Yes."

"So let me ask you a few things. And don't answer right away. Just think about the questions."

* **"Can you grow revenue and enhance customer service while continuing to cut costs at the rate you are right now?"**

* **"Can you enhance customer service by emphasizing the same behaviors that you are right now?"**

* **"If you want to enhance customer service by developing a deeper relationship with customers, have you adjusted your hiring and people development practices to help you deliver that service?"**

* **"If you want to differentiate the bank by being the most trusted financial advisor, what will have to change in order to ensure customers and employees see that you truly are different? What will convince them that you haven't just created a slogan with no connection to reality?"**

Brian paused and handed Jack the index cards so he could reflect on the questions. While Jack played with the index cards, Brian cleaned his glasses.

"Are you ready for more questions?"

"Probably not. I think I get your point. Going back to your body metaphor, each of these 'organs' is important and each is connected either directly or indirectly to the other. They all play their part in ensuring the health of the whole body and they affect each other."

"I think that sums it up pretty well. And when your 'organs' and other 'body parts' are in sync with each other, your bank will perform better."

"But how do I communicate this to the board? Tom Pinkerton has already told me that the growth plan has to speak to each board member."

"Tell me about your board."

Jack spent the next 20 minutes giving Brian a brief overview of his board members, concentrating on key votes that he felt were indicative of their business philosophies.

"Now tell me more about your team."

Jack spent another 20 minutes answering Brian's questions about his team, using anecdotes from before, during, and after the acquisition.

Brian nodded. "You have a diverse team ... which is a good thing. And by diverse, I mean cognitively diverse."

"What does that mean? Are you talking about filters again?"

"Yes. You remembered." Brian grinned.

Jack leaned back, feeling more relaxed than he had in weeks. "After our last conversation, I was talking to Jill about what you said, and she immediately commented that she could see different filters with Jenny and Rob. They had very different experiences in school. They both did well, but different subjects and activities came easier for each of them."

"That's one of the simplest ways for people to understand the idea of filters. We can easily see the innate differences we have when we think about how we learn differently and how some subjects come easier to certain students than others," Brian affirmed.

"This gets to what Pinkerton was encouraging you to do," Brian continued. "Have a growth plan that speaks to different filters. He didn't use those words, but he knows the principle. You should probably set up a meeting with each board member to review the plan and get their reaction and input. That would give you some helpful feedback and allow you to test their filter. I hate to hustle you out, but I have to meet my next client. I'll walk you to your car."

"Sounds good."

As they walked down the hall, Brian continued. "Most of us — in our good moments — use common sense and follow the Golden Rule. We treat people as we wish to be treated. We also, in some situations, treat people as they wish to be treated. That's uncommon sense."

Jack nodded. "I treat each of my kids differently ... and the same. Jenny likes to talk through possible solutions with us before making a decision. Rob, on the other hand, likes time alone to reflect and then discuss alternatives. I respect those differences and interact differently with my kids because of them."

"If people have different strengths and we want them to use their strengths, why would we treat everyone exactly the same way?" Jack wondered out loud. "To be really understood, we need to speak their language, not ours."

"Exactly."

They stepped into the parking lot.

"So, before you go back inside, let me try to summarize what I'm hearing from you. First, the different perspectives from my team on the growth strategy are actually a good thing because they illustrate the strengths of the team, and we need those strengths in order to have a healthy bank. Second, while those different perspectives are good, they also present a challenge because they're currently out of sync. They're not currently supporting each other."

"Right. And just like your team has different filters, your other employees and customers also share those filters. They see your bank through those filters as well."

"I think it would be helpful to have a visual system that represents all of this. Because I can tell you right now, it will be much easier for me to explain and easier for my team and the board to understand if they have something to look at other than words. Index cards won't do the trick."

"That's a great idea. I have something that you can use." *(You can see what Brian has in mind on pages 55-61.)* "I'll have our communications group tweak it a little bit and put something together before we meet with your team. I also think it would help the team and the board understand how the different aspects of the growth plan fit together by choosing one aspect that is the starting point. In your case, it would be quite natural to return to your original goals in acquiring Liberty Bank: growth and enhanced customer service."

"Or, maybe, now we could view it as growth through better customer service."

"That works, too. So your team's task then becomes identifying how to articulate the other aspects of the growth plan in ways that are in sync with your focus: growth through better customer service. The first would be to identify what better customer service looks like."

"We have a lot of work to do."

"I'll be happy to help you in any way I can."

"You've been a huge help already. I'll have Mary set up meetings for you and me with my team members, and we'll get started."

"Great. I'll send her my calendar."

- Purpose
- Signature Strength
- Stakeholders
- Vision
- Culture
- Process

A Visual Overview:

How the System Works:

This is the visual system that Brian referred to in the preceding conversation with Jack. The following pages describe and illustrate the six building blocks necessary for a sustainable organization to be in sync.

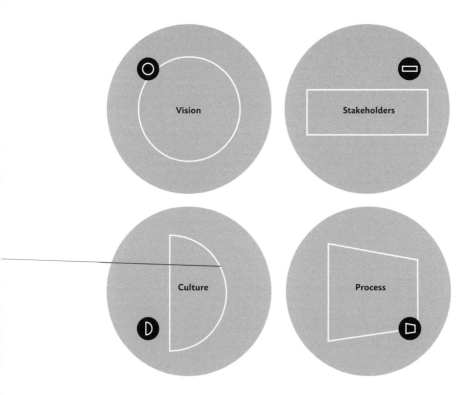

Vision

What is the future state we're trying to create?
What do you think the future state should be?
What direction are we going?

Stakeholders

Who are our key stakeholders and how do we
know what they expect from us?

Culture

What are the values and beliefs that help us toward
our future state?

Process

What do we do (our processes and procedures) that
allows us to claim our signature strength as authentic
and deliver what our key stakeholders need?

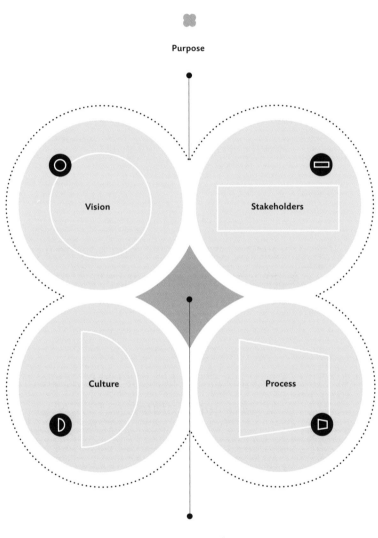

Purpose

Vision

Stakeholders

Culture

Process

Signature Strength

Purpose

Why do we exist? Our purpose provides a context for everything we do.

Signature Strength

How are we different? What makes our organization unique and engender the greatest stakeholder loyalty? Our signature strength differentiates us from our peers and should be woven into everything we do.

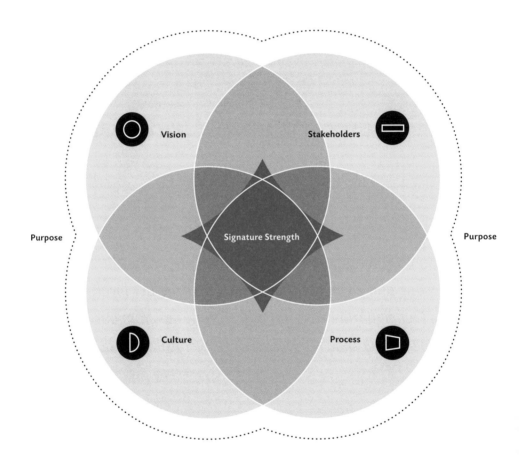

The System in Sync:

Sync occurs when your purpose provides the context for everything you do, your signature strength connects to your vision, stakeholders, culture and processes, and each element of your framework promotes the health and optimal functioning of the entire system.

Each element of your framework continually influences the others and, when in sync, supports the others.

11

The Staff Meeting

The aroma of coffee filled the room as each team member poured a cup and grabbed a Krispy Kreme or bagel. They each took a place around the conference room table and engaged in small talk as they waited for Jack. They knew that part of the staff meeting was dedicated to their input about the growth strategy, and they each had their calendars, as instructed.

Jack strolled in with a smile and took his seat at the head of the table. He poured himself a glass of water and took a sip.

"As you know, I've had conversations with each of you over the last few weeks." He looked around the table. Everyone looked expectant. "They've been very helpful. I appreciate the thought and time you've given to your input."

"It was a good exercise," Kevin said. The others nodded their assent.

"What it all comes down to is that we need to be in sync moving forward. Right now we're out of sync. We need a growth strategy that everyone can relate to. I've met with Brian O'Connor a couple times to help me sort out what I've been hearing. You've all met Brian. He worked with Stuart to develop our talent management approach."

"As I think about my discussions with Brian, I realize that we need to create a framework that we can use in the years ahead to update our growth strategy. We're in crisis mode right now, and we need to address the board's concerns. At the same time, this is an opportunity to create a framework that will be a guiding document for the future. Some things will change, like our vision. Others, such as our purpose or mission, will be more constant."

"Is this something we as a team are going to create?" Pauline asked.

"Yes and no. We will create it, but I think it's imperative to get input from different types of employees. We need everyone's perspective and buy in for this to work. Everyone needs to know that their opinion is valued – even if their views are not implemented – and they need to know their part in the growth strategy. It's harder than just telling everyone what we expect, but it's also more effective."

"So are we in deeper trouble than I thought?" Kevin asked.

"I don't want to be too negative. We are still a highly successful bank. Over the long term we have performed well and made money for all of our stakeholders. We are no different than most other organizations. Sync is something that we need to continually work at especially if we want to create our own future rather than simply be reactive.

"Think of it this way, after the merger we focused on operations making sure everything functioned smoothly. We made sure that all of our employees' benefits were handled well, and we made sure our systems would be consistent from a customer perspective. But I don't think we spent enough time on how the combined organization would need to change to successfully grow and meet our hopes for the future. This is a great time to take measure and plan our future."

"Brian has helped me realize a few things about the nature of our growth strategy and the nature of your personal strengths. So what I want each of you to do, and why I asked you to bring your calendars, is to talk to Mary as you leave and get on my calendar so that each of you can meet with Brian and me. I'll send you a memo after this meeting to outline what our discussion will cover. I've made sure that she knows to make this the top priority for my schedule."

"Any questions? No? Good. Don't forget to stop by Mary's desk on your way out."

"Now for item two on the agenda."

Section III:

The Filters

12

The Futurists

Mary had set up a series of early-morning meetings with each member of Jack's senior team at his favorite coffee shop, Café Lingua. Jack and Brian's goal was to talk informally with each team member about three things:

* **One:** *His or her personal strengths*
* **Two:** *How these personal strengths show up in organizational dynamics*
* **Three:** *Ways to communicate with others who share those strengths*

Austin, the president of Horizon Bank, was up first. He ordered a new latte on the menu, and Jack and Brian decided to take a chance and order the same. They snaked their way, lattes in hand, through the crowd at the café and found a quiet corner table.

Austin knew the goals for the meeting and quickly blurted out, "So, guys, tell me about my strengths."

Jack chuckled and pulled out his notes, glad that Austin had taken the initiative. "Well, Austin," Jack began, "what I've noticed during our recent discussions is your directional focus." He took a sip of the latte. "Not bad. A little too sweet, maybe."

"That's why I like it," Austin said. "Go ahead."

"You need to know what's next. You have an intense interest in the next step. That helps orient you to what is happening at the bank."

Austin nodded and listened closely.

"You may have noticed that other people don't have that need. Kevin certainly doesn't. He wants to focus on developing a process, and he follows that process religiously to make sure the job gets done.

Futurist

Austin

What makes Austin a Futurist?

He looks for what the future does hold or could hold.

"Jack told me that Kevin stressed out after your presentation on the future of banking?" Brian added.

"I remember that well. We had a few tense moments, but we worked through it," Austin acknowledged. "It is frustrating when people don't look up from what they're doing to see the train that is heading right toward us. It may be off in the distance now, but it's coming our way. They don't even hear the whistle blowing."

"Working it out with Kevin was probably more a credit to your maturity than a help to the understanding you could have had if you had stepped back to see what was happening," Brian offered.

"What do you mean?" Austin looked puzzled.

"When you look at the bank you see a horizon. You see either what the future does hold or could hold. Your focus on the horizon and what is happening beyond the bank altered the timeline for your acquisition. And that affected Kevin's to-do list."

Austin nodded.

"It's less important to Kevin where the bank is headed. Kevin sees a series of processes that lead to a horizon, but he's not focused on the horizon. He has a different filter, if you will, than you do. That's why your focus on the future throws him off. He prefers to be the guy who gets things done and helps us improve how you get things done."

Austin nodded again and added, "So, I admit that I think a lot about what is next and our direction. But so what? What do I do with that knowledge? What does that mean for the bank and me? It's not like I think of myself as a visionary. I do try to look at how trends and movements are affecting business, but I'm not out to transform society or the banking industry — although right now I think somebody should be."

"Is it OK if I call you a Futurist?"

"Well, that depends on what it means. It sounds pretty cool."

"There are several kinds of Futurists. First, and the rarest, are true visionaries. They want to change the way we live and interact with one another.

"Secondly, there are those like you who watch trends and think about how to react to movements and shifting attitudes in order to respond well.

"Thirdly, there are those who just want to know where the bank is going.

They don't want to shape a new future or factor in trends. They just want to know what's next. They may just be into the novelty of the next new bright and shiny thing.

"And some of these Futurists like to think about how the pieces fit together into a greater whole. They recognize that every shift in one area of the organization affects another part of the organization."

"And how does this apply to the rest of the bank?" Austin drained his cup.

"Great question," Brian responded. "Since we know there are others like you who need to know what is next, we should learn how to communicate effectively to you and people like you about strategic issues and your identity as an organization."

"Strategic issues like acquisitions," Austin interjected.

"Like acquisitions," Brian affirmed. "Without overgeneralizing or labeling people, we can gauge how each message would sound to a Futurist. These groups that I've talked to Jack about allow us to think about how to communicate with and engage different people."

"So, how do we avoid having people feel like they're being labeled? Why is it important to put me in a category?"

"Well, we don't need to use formal assessments to effectively use this knowledge," Jack interjected. "It's not like we're going to have a label in a personnel file or have people wear different color nametags. What we do know is that there are patterns to our cognitive differences and if we can use those patterns we can help people understand better what our bank's focus is and help them feel more a part of it."

"Let's say we are about to communicate how the acquisition will change certain internal bank processes and operations," Jack continued. "We'll need to address how that helps us move toward the future we hope for the bank and our customers. That would appeal to a Futurist more than just a manual on how specific processes are going to change."

"Futurists are typically not motivated just by quantitative data. In fact, at times, using numbers will shut them down. Communicating with Futurists through stories and metaphors is more helpful."

Austin grinned. "And, in our case, Carter and the board are big bad wolves trying to blow our house down?"

"Maybe." Jack grimaced. "But not if we're ready for them."

"So are we going to try to figure out who the Futurists are so we can communicate with them in the appropriate way?" Austin asked.

"No," Brian responded, "though that can be a next step and appropriate for coaching situations. My hope is that if we apply what we learn about Futurists and take into account their needs for knowing the bank's direction and their communication preferences, they will naturally gravitate to messages and projects that are suited to them."

"So in a coaching context, how would your differences play out since sometimes a Futurist will be coaching someone who isn't?" Austin inquired.

"And other times someone who isn't a Futurist will be coaching a Futurist," Brian added.

"Exactly."

"That's something we can address later. For now, we're simply hoping to introduce these ideas at the highest possible level to see what resonates."

"Great." Austin added with a smile, "It's a future event I can look forward to!"

Austin and Jack both chuckled in tacit acknowledgement that a new corporate language was forming in front of them.

Jack pushed his chair back. "So what do you think?" he asked as they all stood up.

"Well, I'm certainly interested in exploring how to focus more of our strategic communication on our direction. But, you aren't surprised by that, are you?" Austin wadded up his napkin.

"Not really," Jack admitted.

"Seriously, I look forward to learning more about what other people focus on when they look at who we are and where we're going. When is our meeting?"

"A week from Wednesday."

"I'll be there!"

Use Jack's notepad to record thoughts about Futurists in your organization

and how they help you focus on the future.

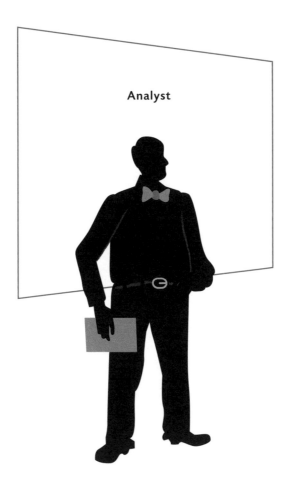

Analyst

Kevin

What makes Kevin an Analyst?
He knows how to get things done.

13

The Analysts

Jack and Brian's next meeting was with Kevin, COO of Horizon Bank. Kevin could pick apart any problem and, unfortunately, many solutions as well. He had a tendency to be so analytical that few initiatives could pass the "Kevin test" as his staff called it.

Kevin piled a doughnut and cinnamon roll onto his plate, and then snagged a cup of cocoa. They found an empty table and Kevin spent a few moments settling into his chair and arranging his favorite indulgences. Jack reminded Kevin of the three goals for the meeting.

"Right," said Kevin, speaking around a mouthful. "Shoot."

"Kevin, you're a great analyst," Jack began. "We're all aware of that. You're able to look at a situation and dissect it into manageable parts for everyone. You like to clearly define goals, are very logical, want specific next steps, and are attentive to the time it takes to achieve things. If I had to pick the archetype of a great project manager, I would choose you."

"Thanks." Kevin interjected.

"You're welcome. You enjoy order and work to create it. You excel at planning, getting things done on time, being attentive to detail, and bringing structure to big projects, where others can't see any. Do you remember when we changed our timeline for this acquisition?"

"Unfortunately, yes, I do remember. It took me a while to adjust."

"You were so focused on moving us forward according to the original timeline that the change was a shock to your system. I remember some pretty heated discussions. While Austin was scouting for trends about where the industry was headed, you were focused on where we had already agreed we were heading. You were plowing ahead full speed."

"Austin is definitely more open to change than I am, and it seems at some times that he seeks it out," Kevin noted. "I think the challenge for Austin is that he doesn't always realize the implications of his ideas. The devil is in the details, and I see the devil very clearly."

"I agree," said Jack.

"Austin's strength is direction and yours is execution," Brian added. "As we described it to him, he's focused on the horizon while you're focused on the steps and processes that lead the bank forward to your horizon. The bank needs both of these strengths in order to be in sync. You and your fellow Analysts provide stability and a certain type of security. There's a confidence that things will get done that is reassuring to others. So, do these observations resonate with you?"

"Definitely," Kevin replied. "For better or worse, that's me. I look at a business as a series of processes that allow us to provide something of value and make money. Efficient processes mean more profit for us and our shareholders."

"So given these general characteristics, how would you recommend we communicate the bank's strategy, Kevin?"

"I've been thinking about this since you sent your e-mail with the agenda for our meeting," Kevin responded, licking sugar off his fingers. "There are three things that I think are helpful."

He ticked them off:

* **Communicate in lists or steps.**
* **Be concrete and specific.**
* **Be brief and efficient.**

"Tell me more." Jack had his pen and notepad ready.

"Communicating in lists helps give us a starting point for our own personal to-do list," Kevin explained. "Since we like closure and getting things done, lists or steps create a ready-made template for us to work from.

"Being concrete and specific keeps us from being annoyed by any whiff we might get of ambiguity. If there is any confusion or wavering, we'll sense it. If you don't know specifically what you want us to do, don't bother giving us direction. For us, ambiguity is like blood to a shark; we'll attack — in an emotionally intelligent way, of course."

"Of course," Jack and Brian responded in unison.

"The same applies to flowery language. We tend to avoid metaphors. For us, life isn't a highway or a journey, or any of those other nebulous things. Life is accomplishing things. It's linear and builds in a logical progression: 1,2,3.

"Think about a process map. It's sometimes the only way you can connect all the dots and make sure things connect. Sometimes ideas sound great, but when you map them, you can see where the faults in logic are."

Kevin finished off his cinnamon roll.

"And, if there is going to be a change, give us time to process it and an opportunity to provide input into how to implement the change. We typically don't trust a person who whipsaws us to come up with an effective way of implementing processes."

"So, can I count on you to help us develop and implement a process for using what we're learning about our strengths, both as a bank and as individuals?" Jack asked.

"Absolutely. After our staff meeting with Brian next week, I'll create a preliminary plan with next steps and a timeline for the team's review."

"Thanks, that would be great." Jack and Brian both left the meeting feeling they had made a major step forward.

ANALYSTS

THE FILTERS

Use Jack's notepad to record thoughts about Analysts in your organization

and how they help you execute your key strategies.

14

The Connectors

Stuart was already at Café Lingua waiting with Jack and Brian's favorite coffees as well as his own when they walked in the door. Stuart had worked with Brian before and was eager to hear what Brian was proposing. Stuart had entered HR from the Organizational Development (OD) side of HR and had an intense interest in how personality differences affect the workplace and organizational performance. After Brian answered some questions about his current projects, Jack cautiously started the dialogue.

"Stuart, this is a bit of a stretch for me, since you know more about maximizing the strengths of people than I do, but I think there's something we can learn from each other that will help the bank."

"I'm sure there is," Stuart interjected.

"You may recall our conversation a while ago about our values and culture."

"Of course." Stuart was stacking and unstacking a collection of spoons. "But we're going to talk about my strengths, right?"

"Yes, but bear with me a minute. I've noticed that the primary filter for some of our employees is a sense of connection to other people. You're an outstanding example of this."

Stuart nodded.

"You have an amazing ability to get groups to work better together. It seems that you're able to do that because you understand the surface dynamics between people. You have a friendly and open style that is very much in the present and focused on resolving issues in a pragmatic and practical way. And you're great in a crisis because you can feel what people are going through in the moment and respond in a way that is attuned to the sensitivities of everyone involved. Am I on track?"

"Yeah, that's me all right. I think Brian and you have done your home-work well."

"Let me add a few other observations," Jack continued. "You are superb at reading a room. You have a sixth sense about what the group mood is in the moment and can turn on a dime to take advantage of group energy or pump up the group when energy is down. How do you do it?"

"I don't know. I just do. I've never tried to analyze how it happens." Stuart laughed.

"You have another quality that's hard to describe," Jack added. "I see it when you make even impersonal tasks feel more comfortable and people-oriented."

Stuart waved at someone across the room before turning his attention back to Jack.

"What do you think the rest of us need to know about communicating with Connectors?" Jack inquired.

"Oh, is that what you're calling me and my tribe?"

"For now."

"Well, you've already mentioned things that I think are pretty important," Stuart responded thoughtfully. "The important thing for Connectors is that we don't create values that are hollow. We're able to see if they don't ring true with employees. So I guess we're the smoke detectors when it comes to potential cultural fires.

"And getting back to your earlier comment, I think we are able to make tasks more comfortable and people-oriented because we like to mix business and pleasure. So, having fun events that communicate a business message are best for us. And we like to initiate them, too!"

Stuart played with the spoons again.

"And since we're doers, the plans may not be perfect like Kevin's would be, but they're close enough and everything seems to get done in spite of the fact that we haven't crossed every 't' and dotted every 'i.'

"Part of the fun of events or games to communicate corporate goals is that things don't happen as planned. Things unfold and spontaneity for us is a good thing. It's what makes life fun!

Connector

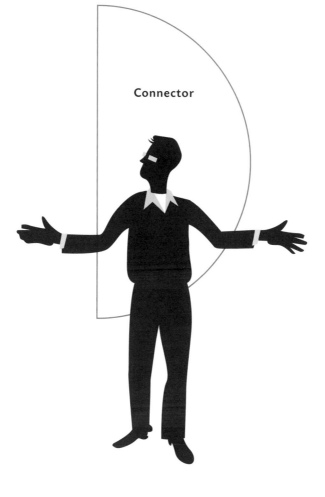

Stuart

What makes Stuart a Connector?

He knows how to rally the troops to focus on shared goals.

"And whatever you do, don't ask us to sit in a room for a lecture. We won't last more than 15 minutes."

"I know the feeling," Jack interjected.

"The payoff for whatever we're communicating needs to be related to promoting teamwork. It has to be about the group — a group goal, relationships within the group, or the group's purpose. With this Liberty Bank acquisition, for example, we needed to be reminded that what we were asked to do would enhance teamwork, or make it easier to work more smoothly with our new colleagues, or help us figure out where we fit in the new and improved Horizon Bank."

"That's very helpful." Jack was busy taking notes. "Anything else?"

"Just make it fun, pragmatic. Let us support group goals and that would be great. We see any organization as a network of people, not as a flow chart."

"Or a set of tasks."

"Right. And not a P&L statement." Stuart grinned. "Now if you don't mind, there's a couple of people over there I want to 'connect with' before I go back to the office.

"Brian, let's schedule lunch soon to catch up more," Stuart offered.

"Sounds good. You call me. I know you've got your hands full right now with the growth plan."

Use Jack's notepad to record thoughts about Connectors in your organization and

how they help you focus on shared organizational priorities and rally the troops.

Interpreter

Pauline

What makes Pauline an Interpreter?

She can see what is unique about customers and employees.

15

The Interpreters

Jack was just getting his coffee when Pauline walked into Café Lingua.

"Go ahead and get a table," she said. "I'll join you in a sec."

A few minutes later Pauline was at the table with her steaming mug. As she sat down, she asked. "So how has your week been?"

"Well, my meetings with the team have been good. I'm a regular here now," Jack said smiling at the barista.

"And how are Jill and the kids?"

"They're doing great. Jenny loves Bowdoin – she's been there six weeks and already feels totally at home. Rob is something of a soccer maniac, and Jill was just asked to serve on the board of the Art Museum."

"She should like that! It fits her personality."

"It's a great fit for her."

As Brian walked into the café, Jack stood up and offered to run up to the counter and order his coffee. "Sorry I'm late. I had to drop my daughter off at school and the drop off line was painfully slow today."

"No problem," Pauline offered. "Let's catch up while Jack gets your coffee."

When Jack came back with Brian's coffee, Brian was just wrapping up his family update for Pauline.

"So how can I help you guys?" Pauline inquired, shifting to the business at hand.

"Well," Jack peered into his coffee cup for a moment. "I'm hoping that you can confirm observations that I've made about you and give me some insight into others who are like you."

"Others like me? What do you mean?"

"Others who see the world through the same filter."

"My filter, eh? How will that help you or our clients?"

"Exactly the kind of questions I'd expect from you." Jack grinned. "Your first thought is always connected to others, especially to a benefit for our stake-holders. You naturally put yourself in the shoes of others."

Pauline nodded. "It's a reflex."

"Now to answer your question of how it helps. Remember the conversa-tion we had last week?"

"Of course. I won't let up on us either."

"And I hope you won't let up," Jack interrupted. "We need you to keep pushing us to have better definition of our key stakeholders and what they value. And that's exactly how this meeting helps. I want you to be clear about your strengths and the ways you contribute to the bank. And I want you to understand how your strengths affect how you view the bank and what we do."

"Go on. Tell me about my strengths."

"Answer this first," Brian chimed in. "How do you view a 'business'? What I mean is, what is it? Be it the bank or another business, describe it for me."

"Good question. Give me a minute." Pauline stirred her coffee. "I see a business as promises and potential," she began thoughtfully. "We have tremen-dous opportunities that are always before us to deliver on both the explicit and implicit promises we make to our stakeholders. And we have people in the bank who are just waiting to use the talents and abilities they have to help deliver those promises. We just need to tap into that potential."

"That's what I'm talking about!" Brian blurted out as he slapped his hand on the table. "That is such a different view of the bank than others have. No one would tell you that your view is wrong, but it's not what comes naturally to the others on the team. It's not what they think of first or what pushes them through their day."

Pauline smiled. "I can't help but think about the bank that way. If I couldn't see the promises and potential lived out, I couldn't work here."

Brian added, "It appears to us that:
* **Kevin:** *sees the bank as a collection of processes that deliver a desired result.*
* **Austin:** *sees the bank as a potential, but in a big picture sense, not a personal sense.*
* **Stuart:** *sees the bank as a web of people connected to each other."*

"That certainly sounds like them," Pauline acknowledged.

"Your strengths help you focus on the needs of individual stakeholders because you are adept at reading the behavior of others through non-verbal cues," Brian continued. "You have a high degree of empathy and patience which suits you well for putting yourself in the place of others.

* "**You know that people are motivated by different things**
* **You know that people think differently**
* **You know that people relate to others differently**
* **You can listen to others without an agenda.**

"And even when your non-verbal radar isn't picking up individual unique-ness instinctively, you can draw it out of people in a way that doesn't make them feel probed or labeled."

"Now that is a pet peeve of mine," Pauline interrupted. " When we label someone, we overlook that person's uniqueness. Kierkegaard said it best,

If you label me you negate me.

"So, I hesitate to mention this part," Jack said sheepishly.

"Go ahead, I can handle it." Pauline grinned.

"Brian has a label for people like you."

Pauline laughed. "Go ahead — if you must. I understand the need for descriptors, just as long as they're used correctly. So, what's my label?"

"Interpreter."

Pauline cocked her head to one side. "Interpreter? How so?"

Well, like Brian said before, you are adept at reading the behavior of others through non-verbal cues," Jack replied. "You look beyond words to behavior and practices. It's someone who knows the importance of walking the talk."

"I can live with that."

"Good. So what about communicating strategy to others like you. How do we translate who we are as an organization to Interpreters?" Jack continued.

"The first thing is that any communication needs to be personal," Pauline advised. "Ideally, we need to offer opportunities for interpersonal interaction. If the message can be delivered in person, that's the best option. If not, then stories or examples are the next best medium.

"And, again, ideally, the communication needs to emphasize our unique value and how it is lived out in the lives of our stakeholders, especially our clients."

Jack nodded. "Pauline, I'm so glad you're on the team. This is a link we really need."

Use Jack's notepad to record thoughts about Interpreters in your

organization and how they help you notice unique

characteristics of key customers and employees and tailor value.

Section IV:

From Clarity to Congruence

16

The Path to Being in Sync

Brian was the person people barely noticed when he was in a room. Until he spoke. Then the words that came out of his mouth impressed people with their ability to strike at the heart of any issue. He was a small, unassuming man – thin and lean from the miles he spent training for marathons, with wispy hair and round, wire-rimmed glasses.

Jack had asked Brian to be part of an expanded weekly meeting for his senior team. He wanted an outsider with credentials to talk to his team about the connection between strengths and the identity of the bank.

After Jack's brief introduction, Brian started the session. "I want everyone to grab a pen or pencil and a sheet of paper. Now with your weaker hand – if you're right-handed use your left hand and vice versa – sign your name. Write your name on the paper like you're signing a letter.

Brian paused a few moments and watched as the team members signed their names.

"How did that feel?" Brian asked when they all had finished.

"Frustrating. Hard." offered one team member.

"Awkward," added another.

"I had to think first before I started writing," another chimed in.

"Good. Now, write your name with your stronger hand," Brian requested. "Again, just like you're signing a letter."

After each person finished, he asked, "How did that feel?"

"Natural and smooth," a team member started.

"Easy," someone said.

"Familiar. A relief. Like putting on my favorite pair of slippers after a long day on my feet," added another.

Try this exercise by signing your name with your **weaker hand** below:

Now, try signing your name with your **stronger hand** below:

"So what does this exercise tell us?" Brian asked.

"That I'm thankful I've never hurt my right hand," Pauline offered.

The team chuckled and looked at each other, expecting someone else to be the first to offer a serious answer.

"Notice the language I used," Brian hinted. "I referred to your stronger and weaker hands."

"Well, we were told this meeting had two topics:

"One: *Our input on the growth strategy we need to develop for the next board meeting.*

"Two: *The meetings we've had with Jack and you regarding our strengths.*

"So, I'm going to go out on a limb and say that you're trying to illustrate something about our strengths," Kevin suggested.

"Absolutely," Brian affirmed, "so what am I trying to illustrate?"

Silence.

Brian broke the silence by saying, "It's very simple, but not necessarily obvious or easy to live. We all know that we have strengths and weaknesses. Working within our strengths is more natural and takes less effort, thought, and energy than working within our weaknesses. It's not that we can't work in our areas of weakness. It's just not as easy or as effective."

"In applying this principle to the bank, I would suggest that you continue to develop a greater awareness of what your strengths and weaknesses are and, as a team, be aware of what each person brings to the party."

"In addition — and this is the most important point for today — you need to be aware that these strengths and weaknesses have an effect not only on how you do your job and what your role in the bank should be, but on how you connect with the identity of the bank. Jack, could you flip on the projector?"

Jack dimmed the lights and turned on the LCD projector in the middle of the conference room table. The following image appeared ...

"Now, write down on a piece of paper what you see." Brian waited while they each recorded what they saw.

"So what did you see, Kevin?" Brian asks.

"A Greek Revival building."

"That's what I see," Pauline volunteered.

"I see profiles of businessmen," Stuart interjected.

"Me too. But I've seen it before," Jack admitted.

"I saw both. I'm not sure which I saw first. It was so fast," Pete added.

"My point in using this illustration is not which one is seen first but this: Both images are there, yet most people only see one until someone points out the other image. The columns or the human profiles. And one may be easier to see than the other, but they are both there and are essential to the whole picture.

"It's a limited analogy, but it is comparable to what people see when they look at Horizon Bank. Some may just see the processes and procedures. Others may most easily see the end result, the value to the customer."

"So when I see the future of the bank — nonpsychically of course — others can be oblivious to its very presence?" Austin queried.

"Exactly," Brian affirmed.

"That would be me," Kevin laughed.

"And conversely, the processes and procedures of the bank are just 'profiles of businessmen' to me," Austin suggested.

"Right."

Brian entertained questions for the next 15 minutes about implications for the bank as it relates to employee attraction and retention until Jack brought the discussion to a conclusion.

"Brian is making himself available after our meeting if we want to explore this further," Jack interjected. "But for the sake of time I want to move on to the next steps of our growth strategy preparation for the board.

"So what are we going to do to get more clarity for what we want to present to the board? As you know, I've hired Brian to facilitate a process that will help us better articulate what we stand for. That process will begin at next month's offsite, which will include several of our board members.

"Brian has created a simple visual expression of what we've been hearing and here it is. This will be our framework — our guiding document — going forward. We have some gaps to fill in, and it will take some time for us to do that. But it's the only way to ensure that we're in sync. *(Refer to pages 55-61.)*

"I know that some of you will need some time to process this. You may not naturally think about frameworks or models. But it's fairly simple. We will discuss the framework more when we work through it at the offsite, but for now think about it as a series of questions:

* "**Vision:** *What is the future state we're trying to create? What do you think the future state should be? What direction are we going?*
* **Signature strength:** *How are we different than our peers? Should we be developing a different signature strength for the future? If so, what should it be?*
* **Purpose:** *Why do we exist as an organization?*
* **Stakeholder:** *Who are our key stakeholders and how do we know what they expect from us?*
* **Culture:** *What are the values and beliefs that help us toward our future state?*
* **Process:** *What do we do (our processes and procedures) that allows us to claim our signature strength as authentic and deliver what our key stakeholders need?"*

"So Jack, I think the Board will be glad that we're addressing these questions," Kevin interjected. "And I think including them at our offsite makes sense so they can be part of the process. It seems though that they probably will want more detail than just the answers to these questions. Where will the operational plan come from?"

"You're exactly right," Jack acknowledged. "After we address the more strategic aspects of our framework we'll be addressing the tactical steps to make it come alive so that we can get the financial results we've promised our stakeholders. And we'll address how to do that at the end of next month's offsite. The process aspect of the framework will be the starting point for creating an operational growth plan. And having all of these elements in our growth plan, we'll be sure to speak to the concerns of all our board members and stakeholders.

"Any more questions for now?" Jack paused and smiled.

"We have a lot of work ahead of us. To be in sync and get the financial results the board expects — and our shareholders expect — we need to get all aspects of the bank aligned — our direction, culture, signature strength, processes, and purpose. And we need to translate our identity in ways that resonate with our employees, customers, and other stakeholders.

"I'm confident that as a team we can lead the bank into the next phase of our history with a renewed sense of purpose and direction, a vibrant and healthy culture, and increase value for all of our stakeholders."

A Visual Overview of Horizon Bank:

Representations of the Current State (A) and Future State (B) of Horizon Bank

The illustration at left represents the current state of Horizon Bank: purpose, culture, and vision are more in sync than the other elements.

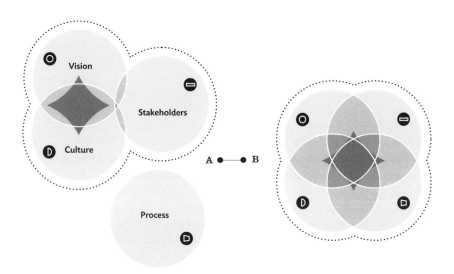

The illustration at right represents the future of Horizon Bank after Jack and his team get the bank's signature strength, stakeholders, and process in sync with other elements.

17

The End ... and Your Beginning

Just in case you were wondering, and we hope you were, Jack kept his job. There was healthy debate within his team about the growth plan. There was also debate at the Board meeting. Not all of it was healthy, but it was debate nonetheless. The Board recommended some modifications that Jack's team will integrate, and Jack and his team survived to live another day at Horizon Bank.

Of course, the Board expected detailed progress updates at every Board meeting, and Carter continued to be Jack's most aggressive antagonist. But the Board appreciated the initiative that Jack and his team demonstrated in bringing a fresh approach to developing a growth plan.

Jack chose to start by clearly defining the bank's key customers and he built the rest of the growth strategy around it. In choosing to focus on stakeholder value, he was required to ask himself and his team the following questions:

*How do we best describe our value to
our stakeholders?*

*How well are we delivering that value?
How do we know? If there are gaps in our delivery,
how will we bridge those gaps?*

*How well do our behaviors and beliefs help us
deliver value to stakeholders?*

*Do we need to change the way we treat each
other as fellow employees?*

*Do we need to change the way we treat our
customers? Our suppliers? Our shareholders?*

*How well do our plans for the future align with
our projections of stakeholder expectations?*

*What aspect of our organization is unique or best
in class and how do we capitalize on it?*

Section V:

Epilogue

But, enough of Jack's story. What is your story?

If you want to promote sync in your organization, how will you make progress? Your questions will be different because you may need to develop a vision for what your organization needs to look like in 5 years. Or you may need to clearly differentiate yourself. Your starting point may differ from Jack's, and, therefore, your growth plan will look different.

At Dialect, Inc. our belief is that organizations that know what they stand for and live it are better positioned to succeed. While thinking about "what you stand for" may seem too conceptual for some, it has practical, everyday implications. When what you stand for is woven throughout your entire organization it promotes focus, commitment, and helps everyone make decisions that benefit your organization and your stakeholders.

Regardless of the specific needs of your organization, if Jack's story resonated with you, we hope that you'll take the next step and do one of three things:

1.

If you identify more with Section I, The System, then ask yourself the following questions:

What areas of our growth strategy do we need to work on to get in sync?
Do we need a clearer picture of where we're going?
Do we need to build a different culture?
Do we need a better way to differentiate our organization?
Do we need to clarify our purpose?
Do we need to clarify our key stakeholders and more clearly define what they need?
Do we need to create different processes and better invest resources to support our growth strategy?

2.

If you identify more with Section III, The Filters, then ask yourself the following questions:

How does my leadership style affect who we are as an organization?

Am I more directional or operational?

Do I focus more on what helps the group or do I focus more on what makes each person and/or customer unique?

How do my answers to those questions affect who we are as an organization?

Do my answers help me see potential gaps in our growth strategy?

3.

Maybe your growth strategy is in sync and you've factored in how your own filter affects your leadership style, but your employees and/or customers are viewing your organization very differently than you do. You need to make your growth strategy come alive; you need to translate your growth strategy in ways that connect with your stakeholders. Start by asking yourself the following questions:

How should we communicate, reinforce, and measure the effectiveness of our growth strategy with those who...

Think about direction first?

Think about group dynamics and culture first?

Think about process and/or metrics first?

Think about stakeholders first?

After choosing which of these three options is best for you,
if you want more help, we are available for:

organizational assessments

speaking engagements and workshops

consulting

www.dialect.com | p: (314) 863-4400

About the Authors

photo by Brian Cassidy

Andy Kanefield *is the founder and CEO of Dialect, Inc. Dialect helps CEOs and presidents manage the relationships between divisions or departments in order to achieve sync. Dialect does this through recognizing the impact of cognitive diversity — we are each wired differently, motivated by different parts of an organization's identity.*

The genesis of Dialect, Inc. was an integration of what Andy learned as the parent of a son, Parker, with special needs and as a partner in an advertising agency.

As a parent, Andy researched the latest developments in neuroscience, learned about innate strengths, and noticed certain patterns in our cognitive wiring.

As an advertising executive, Andy noticed that often organizations weren't wired to deliver what they promised to customers and were often out of sync internally because there was no intentional, coherent system that tied departments and people together.

The integration of a systems perspective for organizations and the built-in filters of individuals led to the development of a model for promoting organizational sync.

Andy was a partner in a branding company for 14 years and is currently a member of TED (Technology, Entertainment and Design). Andy served for many years on the board of Earthways, an environmental education and consulting organization, served as President of the St. Louis chapter of the American Association of Advertising Agencies, and was on the marketing committees of the Missouri Botanical Garden and the Belle Center, a non-profit agency dedicated to facilitating the inclusion of children with special needs and their families into their communities.

Andy received his B.A. in Sociology from the University of Colorado and has completed behavioral training from the nationally-recognized Judevine Center.

You can contact Andy at andy@dialect.com

About the Authors

Mark Powers *has been a consultant with Dialect since 2004. Prior to that he worked for corporations and non-profit organizations in several different roles including relationship manager, career consultant, teacher, and engineer. Mark learned the principles of uncommon sense while working with a remarkable group of high school and college students in Moscow. He enjoys helping people recognize their strengths, connect their strengths to organizational goals, and find meaning in their work.*

He is a member of the National Career Development Association (NCDA) and the St. Louis Organization Development Network (ODN).

Mark earned his B.S. in Electrical Engineering from the University of Illinois and graduated with an M.A. in Counseling from Covenant Theological Seminary.

You can contact Mark at mark@dialect.com

photo by Brian Cassidy

Acknowledgements

We are grateful for the many people who have contributed to the creation of this book. We would especially like to thank the following:

Dan Pink for lending his considerable name to this book.

David Frigstad for his kind words about the book and for his commitment to helping companies develop their growth strategies.

Karin Soukup for being a great partner in helping us visually bring these concepts to life with her thoughtful reflection on the reader's experience and her exceptional design talent.

Betty Burnett for editing Jack's story in a way that brought it to life, and to Mary Menke for helping us dot our i's and cross our t's.

Dan Zettwoch for giving our characters personality through his illustrations.

For our clients, past and present, who help us learn better ways to promote sync.

Terry Bader, David Frigstad, Jim Holbrook, Ellen Krout, Tammy Lamb, Scott Mannis, Joe Osborn, Gordon Philips, Jeff Robinson, and Donna Smith for reviewing rough drafts and providing key insights and help. Any flaws in this book are ours, not theirs.

Finally, and most importantly, we would each like to thank our families:

Lois, who gives me the gifts of wisdom, true love, and the encouragement to go for it and Perry and Parker who teach me every day. I couldn't love you more.

I could accomplish nothing without the love, insight, and support of my wife, Valerie. And to our wonderful children, Jonathan and Emma, 'Thank You!' In our quest to live meaningful lives, you have been our best guides.

www.dialect.com